Root English

Book 3

Wayside School

is Falling Down

Toem Books

John Stephen Knodell

ISBN – 978-4-908152-14-6

Toem Books
Tel. 011-839-3771
Email. info@to-em.com

札幌市中央区北２条西２６丁目２番１８号２６**WEST**ビル　**４F　Room A**

to-em.com

Dedicated to

Yurika & Atsuno

How to Use the Book

The Roots English series is a content-based textbook that uses authentic readings with grammar, writing, and speaking exercises. While the textbook is rich with grammar exercises, exercises can be used to A) create conversations from the grammar exercises B) test students on the problematic grammar points throughout the book, and C) connect the reading book with sections of the textbook, for example, the making perfect sentences and grammar focus sections.

For classes studying English approximately 3-4 hours a week, try to finish one reading section, one grammar focus/preposition/article exercise, and one writing assignment. Each week, test students on one of the grammar exercises, have a review test of the vocabulary, and always use the textbook as an opportunity to speak with students. In order to prepare for writing essays, debate the topic before giving the assignment for homework.

About the Author

John Stephen Knodell has an M.Ed. in TESOL, and has been an English language teacher for over 20 years. He has taught students from 2 years old to students over 80, from private classes to classes of over 100 students. He currently teaches at a university in Japan.

Table of Contents

Reading Section

A Package for Mrs. Jewls

CHAPTER 1

VOCABULARY TO LEARN

frowned, a mess, junk, pass out, sighed, honked, horn, disturbing, interrupted, changed my

mind, grunted, fragile, fortunately, by heart, squashing, mushrooms, huffed, groaned,

sore, gravity, a spelling bee, a grip, numb, collapsed

QUESTIONS

1. Why was Louis a mess?

2. What did Louis lie about?

3. Was the package heavy? Explain.

4. How did Mrs. Jewls pick the person who opened the door?

5. What did Mrs. Jewls do with the package?

Mark Miller

CHAPTER 2

VOCABULARY TO LEARN

cowbell, show-and-tell, weirdo, mention, to correct, discipline, cringed, charged out,

shrugged, a low rumble, can't miss it, a stack of, indignantly, frowned

QUESTIONS

1. Why didn't Benjamin tell Mrs. Jewls about his real name?

2. Why did Todd get into trouble?

3. How do you know the students liked Benjamin?

4. What bad thing happened to Ben because he didn't tell Mrs. Jewls his name?

5. Was Benjamin a nice guy? Explain.

Bebe's Baby Brother

CHAPTER 3

VOCABULARY TO LEARN

pass back, nervously, except for, lately, past midnight, sighed with relief, sternly,

hippopotamus, ray gunn, snuck into, batch of, slave, oatmeal, leaks out, angel, wrecking,

ear plugs

QUESTIONS

1. What was going to happen to Bebe if she didn't do better at school?

2. What did Bebe love about Mrs.Jewls?

3. When did Bebe's brother write on her paper?

4. Did Bebe's parents like Ray?

5. Why was Mrs. Jewls giving Bebe an A+?

6. What is the lie in this story?

Homework

CHAPTER 4

VOCABULARY TO LEARN

fractions, decimals, patiently, didn't match, bewilderment, arithmetic, groaned, broccoli,

explode, pretend, assign it

QUESTIONS

1. Why do you think Mrs. Jewls didn't pick Mac?

2. What was Mac's problem?

3. Why didn't Mac wear another sock?

4. Who knew how Mac's sock got into his refrigerator?

5. Why didn't Nancy have any books?

6. Why did Mac always have so much homework?

Another Story about Socks

CHAPTER 5

VOCABULARY TO LEARN

a hobo, a scraggly beard, stains, patches, spare change, didn't believe in socks, pigtails,

stew, proudly, cannibals, cannonballs, Albert Einstein, weekly

QUESTIONS

1.   How did the hobo take showers?

2.   Why didn't the hobo wear socks?

3.   What was the hobo proud of when he was a student?

4.   Was he a bad child? Explain.

5.   What is Mulligan Stew?

6.   How do we know the students wanted to do well on the test?

Pigtails

CHAPTER 6

VOCABULARY TO LEARN

immature, rushed, teachers' lounge, you're sick, in disgust, waggle, bashed, toppled out,

stared in horror, brick, an extension cord, winced, yelped, dangled, at last, jutted out, the

windowsill, sore

QUESTIONS

1. Who felt great when Leslie's pigtails were pulled?

2. Do you think Paul had a problem with pulling Leslie's pigtails? Explain.

3. Who bothers you in your class? Give an example.

4. What made Paul fall out the window?

5. What would you do if you were going to fall out a window?

Freedom

CHAPTER 7

VOCABULARY TO LEARN

crumbled, oddly, a cage, birdbrain, reluctantly, eased, creaky, echoed, lurking, damp room,

out-stretched, untied, slime, attaché case, regretted, a fake name, chirped, foreign,

definitely

QUESTIONS

1. When did Myron's bird come to the window?

2. Why did Myron sit on the floor?

3. When did Myron go into the basement?

4. Who did he think was down in the basement?

5. Why did Myron want to be free?

6. Would you like to have a bird as a pet? Why or why not?

The Best Part

CHAPTER 8

VOCABULARY TO LEARN

adorable, big deal, commanded, typical, rules, cooed, let you off, a crank, floppy ears,

fangs, cheeks, grim, lap, a carton of, a straw, just might make it

QUESTIONS

1. What happened to students who were bad 3 times in Mrs. Jewls's class?

2. How did Todd's toy get on the floor?

3. Why did Todd get to erase his name off the board?

4. How did the dog change?

5. How did Joy bother Todd?

6. What was the best part about the dog?

Mush

CHAPTER 9

VOCABULARY TO LEARN

mush, wiped, apron, warmed her heart, slice of, ordered the food, left over, tears of joy,

dumped a hot lump, tray, cash register, news quickly spread, immune to it, the goop, his

face flushed, throw up, a mixture of

QUESTIONS

1. Why didn't anybody like to eat Miss Mush's food?

2. How long was the mushroom special sold to students?

3. Why didn't Louis get sick when he ate the food?

4. How did the mushroom special taste?

5. What did it make Ron do when he ate it?

6. Do you like to eat all food, or are you a picky eater?

Music

CHAPTER 10

VOCABULARY TO LEARN

kickball, unfortunately, a tambourine, pass out (give), a triangle, invented, glockenspiel,

bongo drums, snared, eardrums, cymbal, gong, hollered, charged toward each other,

screeched to a halt, musician, principal

QUESTIONS

1. Why did Benjamin like being Mark more?

2. What was bad about the music?

3. Why couldn't Mrs. Jewls hear Benjamin?

4. What happened when the principal complained about the noise?

5. If you could play any instrument well, which one would it be?

Kathy and D.J.

CHAPTER 11

VOCABULARY TO LEARN

splat, jolly, felt like, quit, except, sighed, snap out of it, stared, headed on up, burst out

laughing, jerk, delight, ground you, allowance, triumphantly, choke, frown, wrist

QUESTIONS

1. Why did Louis feel sad?

2. Why was Kathy so happy?

3. What made DJ feel so sad?

4. What was a little strange about DJ?

5. Was Kathy happy when DJ gave her his watch?

Pencils

CHAPTER 12

VOCABULARY TO LEARN

chewed, on purpose, slobbered, a disgusting habit, forehead, orchestra, looked at it in

horror, pre-tended, contained, stuffed, keep his promise, instead, held firm

QUESTIONS

1. Who was the 2nd person to give Jason a pencil?

2. What part of his mouth did he use to chew pencils?

3. Why couldn't Rondi bite her pencil?

4. How did Mrs. Jewls solve Jason's eating problem?

5. What did Mrs. Jewls want to do all the time?

6. What is one of your bad habits?

A Giggle Box, Leaky Faucet, and a Fog horn

CHAPTER 13

VOCABULARY TO LEARN

wise, a giggle box, a leaky faucet, a plumber, tears streaming down, teasing, laughed

hysterically, stinky, onrushing car, sobbed, foghorn

QUESTIONS

1. Why did Dana hate stories?

2. Why did the students call Dana 'Leaky Faucet'?

3. How did stories about animals usually end in Mrs. Jewls' class?

4. What did Dana worry about at the end of the story?

5. What makes you sad?

6. Do you ever cry?

Calvin's Big Decision

CHAPTER 14

VOCABULARY TO LEARN

decision, trade, a tattoo, a tutu, once you get, change your mind, giggled like a maniac, his

cheek, an anchor, stuffed up, ankle, soaring

QUESTIONS

1. What was the best part of Calvin's party?

2. What is the problem with Calvin's tattoo?

3. If you were going to get a tattoo, what would it be?

4. What important question did Calvin's father ask him?

She's Back

CHAPTER 15

VOCABULARY TO LEARN

hiccupped, trembling, the water fountain, the banister, a shiver of fear, especially,

nightmares, wastepaper basket, trash, shook with fear, tightly, somewhat hard, my

shadow, right side up

QUESTIONS

1. Why was Deedee screaming?

2. What does a hippo do when it is angry?

3. Who is the meanest teacher in your school?

4. Do you think Louis was a good student in school? Explain.

5. How did Louis's mother know if he was bad at school?

6. Why did Deedee hold Louis's hand?

Love and a Dead Rat

CHAPTER 16

VOCABULARY TO LEARN

bounced off, blushed, assured, accused, for support, prove it, I'll show you, snowflakes,

felt rot-ten, grading papers, disgusting

QUESTIONS

1. How did you know Dameon was in love?

2. How did Dameon show his love for Mrs. Jewls?

3. Did anybody know about Dameon's love for Mrs. Jewls?

4. What did Joy tell Dameon to do to prove that he didn't love Mrs. Jewls?

5. Why did Dameon tell Mrs. Jewls that he loved her?

6. What did Mrs. Jewls teach him about love?

What

CHAPTER 17

VOCABULARY TO LEARN

good point, unless, giggle box, hysterically, made a face, prune juice, griped, caught her

breath, charged up the stairs, a very bumpy ride, grumbled

QUESTIONS

1. Why was Jenny late?

2. Why couldn't Jenny hear Mrs. Jewls?

3. Why didn't Jenny laugh when Mrs. Jewls finished the story?

4. What kind of stories did Jenny like?

5. What was purple?

6. What is different about this story?

The Substitute

CHAPTER 18

VOCABULARY TO LEARN

high marks, glumly, started up the stairs, substitute, courage, unlock, bonkers,

spectacles, ponytail, pass it on, correct, boldly, stated proudly, snickered, giggled,

hysterical, certainly, a genius, closely, as a result, crowded, pleaded

QUESTIONS

1. What did Mark want to do today?

2. Why were the students so happy to have a substitute teacher?

3. Why did Benjamin feel sorry for her?

4. What did Terrence do for the first time all year?

5. Do you think the teacher really knew the students were joking with her?

6. Why did the students learn so much?

A Bad Case of Sillies

VOCABULARY TO LEARN

bad case, sillies, crammed, scurrying, charging up, leaned, stamped, jammed, grunted,

windbreaker, too pooped to, pestering, folded her hands, shark, nudge, a show-off, settle

down, took roll, absent, get off my case, buzzard face, demanded, exclaimed, protested,

streamed down, sternly

QUESTIONS

1. Why did Allison like the quiet stairs?

2. Who was Ms. Zarves?

3. Why was Allison upset at Ron and Deedee?

4. Why did Jason name his goldfish 'Shark'?

5. Was everybody pretending not to hear Allison?

6. What happened to Allison at the end of the chapter?

A Wonderful Teacher

VOCABULARY TO LEARN

arranged, clusters, a singsong voice, on purpose, a million, in alphabetical order,

cheerfully, big deal

QUESTIONS

1. Why did Virginia think Mrs. Zarves was a nice teacher?

2. How long has Virginia studied in Mrs. Zarve's class?

3. Did Nick or Virginia remember where they came from?

4. What did Mrs. Zarves ask the students to do?

5. Why don't they have any homework in Mrs. Zarve's class?

6. How did Allison forget about Mrs. Jewl's class?

Forever is Never

VOCABULARY TO LEARN

stuck, with relief, former, felt a chill run up her spine, punish, experts, announced,

shivered, it all came together, assigns, who knew what she might have up her sleeve, take

a chance, furious, jammed, grunted, pooped, sat with their heads flat

QUESTIONS

1. How many days had Allison been in Miss Zarves's class?

2. What didn't she want to forget?

3. Who did Allison think Miss Zarves could be?

4. What was Miss Zarves's plan?

5. How did Allison act in the class?

6. What is strange about the ending of the story?

Eric, Eric, & Eric

Vocabulary to Learn

crackled, at once, trembled, took a couple of breaths, boomed, bare, crackled his knuckles,

the hard way, one way or another, pounded, stammered, turned pale, scowled, bellowed,

gulped, so long as, slyly, tetherball, resound, neat and trim, come clean

Questions

1. How many Erics were in Mrs. Jewl's class?

2. Was Mr. Kidswatter really angry?

3. Tell me one question Mr. Kidswatter asked one of the Erics.

4. How did Eric Ovens feel in Mr. Kidswatter's office?

5. How does Eric Bacon write?

6. Who do you think told lies to Mr. Kidswatter?

Teeth

CHAPTER 23

VOCABULARY TO LEARN

thanks for nothing, stormed away, scowled, crawled into the bushes, twirled, multi-colored

mustache, winked at, lit up, drop dead, ketchup head, retorted, impressed, you are asking

for it, gleamed, took a vote, ducked just in time

QUESTIONS

1. What was Rondi's problem?

2. Why was Deedee upset?

3. What did Louis refuse to do to Rondi?

4. How did Louis want to help Rondi?

5. Why did Rondi decide to keep her teeth?

6. What is a theme in this story?

Another Story about Potatoes

CHAPTER 24

VOCABULARY TO LEARN

a large glop of, plopped, mound, squirted, squiggly lines, dollops, polka dots, sec-onds,

lumpy, gooey, swirling, creation, abruptly, a frown, terror, utensils, shoveled

QUESTIONS

1. Why did Miss Mush throw away the Mushroom Surprise?

2. What did Sharie eat?

3. What did Joe put on his potato salad?

4. What didn't Bebe know about Joe?

5. What did Joe decide to do with his lunch?

6. What is a theme in this chapter?

A Story That Isn't about Socks

CHAPTER 25

VOCABULARY TO LEARN

dressed up, trousers, vest, polka dots, remained, bikini, wrinkled, a Hawaiian shirt, chokes,

tightened, a toga, bulged, groaned, it's what underneath that counts

QUESTIONS

1. Why did the kids laugh at Stephen?

2. What couldn't he do in the suit?

3. Why wasn't he supposed to sit down?

4. What didn't he like about his clothes?

5. Have you ever worn a suit?

6. Who looked the best, and why?

The Mean Mrs. Jewels

CHAPTER 26

VOCABULARY TO LEARN

bursting, eventually, yardstick, capital, vat, brine, demonstration, frowned, that does it,

snapped, keep still, meekly, slammed down, mocking voice, shriveled up, warts, aisles,

glaring, dared, gulped, a wild guess, return the favor, drenching, froze in ter-ror, blinked

QUESTIONS

1. Who told Mrs. Jewls to give the students lots of work?

2. Why did Mrs. Jewls want to teach 3 new things every day?

3. How are pickles made?

4. What had Mrs. Jewls never told anyone before?

5. Why did Mrs. Jewls go home early?

6. Would you like to be a teacher? Why or why not?

Lost and Found

CHAPTER 27

VOCABULARY TO LEARN

lost and found, shrugged, exclaimed, coughed, split, robbed a bank, murder, tether-ball

pole, get lost, claims, blubbered, proudly

QUESTIONS

1. Why couldn't Maurecia find her lunch?

2. What did Maurecia need with her sandwich?

3. Why don't Joy want Maurecia to tell Louis about the money?

4. How long did Maurecia have to wait to get the money?

5. Why did Joy think she should get something from Mr. Finch?

6. What is a theme in this chapter?

Valoosh

CHAPTER 28

VOCABULARY TO LEARN

indeed, cooties, warts, settle down, sarcastically, breakdancer, grace, classical ball-room dancing, except,

blackmailing, lampshade, or else, bellowed, Gypsies, tango, stomped, somersault, the rear end

QUESTIONS

1. What was the wonderful news?

2. Why didn't anyone want to dance?

3. Why did the students think Myron didn't have to learn dance?

4. What was fun about dancing with Miss Valooosh?

5. What kind of dance were they going to learn the next week?

6. Who was your favourite character in this chapter, and why?

The Lost Ear

CHAPTER 29

VOCABULARY TO LEARN

mammals, determined, report cards, barber, sew, hippie, ambulance, operating room,

whale, hobo, show-and-tell, choke, weirdos, mumbled

QUESTIONS

1. What do you know about mammals?

2. Why did Benjamin have to tell Mrs. Jewls his real name?

3. What was funny about Mac's story?

4. Why did Mark feel good about being in that class? \

5. Where were the bathrooms?

6. What is the plot in this story?

Wayside School is Falling Down

VOCABULARY TO LEARN

whooshed, directly, teetered, tottered back, sway back and forth, crammed, a fire drill,

planted their feet firmly, monitor, constantly, trapdoor, rescue, funnel shaped, violently,

rumble, heeded, cowed, starving, bales of hay, calves, temporarily, pleaded, mooed

QUESTIONS

1. Why was Kathy happy?

2. What do people do in a fire drill?

3. What is the setting in this story?

4. What made the cows come into the school?

5. What is the plot in this story?

6. Why was Wayside School closed?

7. What is a theme in this story?

8. Who is your favourite character in this book, and why?

9. Would you like to read the next Sideways Stories book?

10. What was the atmosphere or mood in this book?

Grammar Focus Section

Grammar Focus 1

ALL OF THE SENTENCES BELOW HAVE MISTAKES. TRY TO CORRECT THE SENTENCES, AND MAKE THEM **PERFECT**.

1. I like dog because it friendly.

2. While I went to school, I was eating a pizza.

3. If I am a monkey, I will eating banana.

4. I slowly walking to work when I meet my Korean, nice friend.

5. On Christmas, I buy present to Hana, but she is happy.

6. Car is small then elephants.

7. I have a Japanese, purple, old car.

8. I was wanting piece of cheeses 2 day ago.

9. She can't cooks a chicken very good.

10. He sad because he don't have friend.

Grammar Focus 2

ALL OF THE SENTENCES BELOW HAVE MISTAKES. TRY TO CORRECT THE SENTENCES, AND MAKE THEM PERFECT.

1. As soon as I will go to home, I will play computer.

2. He is tallest people in class.

3. They study hardly, so they teacher is a happy.

4. Day before yesterday is Sunday.

5. She go to shopping every other days.

6. Every of book in my bag are new.

7. Every students in this class are smart.

8. One of my book are made by gold.

9. Wash dishes are not interested.

10. I like teach you because you sometime are funny.

Grammar Focus 3

ALL OF THE SENTENCES BELOW HAVE MISTAKES. TRY TO CORRECT THE SENTENCES, AND MAKE THEM **PERFECT**.

1. All of people in Earth has a parents.

2. The young guy in mine class has long hairs.

3. I doesn't like a cat, but I am thinking they are kindly.

4. If I tired, I slept.

5. I can reading many information on internet.

6. I like go to downtown because it is many people.

7. Would you to like a water?

8. On the hot day, the people eats ice cream.

9. I was played golfing last Friday, but I didn't played good.

10. When I was elementary school, I study a lots at my room.

Grammar Focus 4

ALL OF THE SENTENCES BELOW HAVE MISTAKES. TRY TO CORRECT THE SENTENCES, AND MAKE THEM **PERFECT**.

1. Rice are good for people's healthy.

2. I am having a sister, and she is a pretty.,

3. I can't doing my homeworks because I am difficult.

4. He run fastly, so I can't catching him.

5. I have cold, so I can't go school yesterday.

6. I am interested at tennis, but I don't play the tennis.

7. Right now, I drink a tea and eat a spaghetti.

8. It take me 5 minutes for washing my a hair.

9. When I do soccer, I enjoy to wear short pants.

10. She is so nice lady, and she smile is nice , too.

Grammar Focus 5

ALL OF THE SENTENCES BELOW HAVE MISTAKES. TRY TO CORRECT THE SENTENCES, AND MAKE THEM **PERFECT**.

1. I heard song on radio, and I dance at my friend.

2. I doesn't have nothing in mine pocket

3. Playing sports are funny because sports is excited.

4. I get up early last morning because I hungry.

5. I wish I have a library in front my home.

6. She don't like to fishing because of boring.

7. I eat always rice at the night.

8. Before sleep, I brush my tooth in a bathroom.

9. I have a plenty of books on my room.

10. I hope I could visit to Kyoto.

Grammar Focus 6

1. I'm play baseball on the park every days..

2. He walk slow, so he nickname is Turtle.

3. I born in Japan, but I can speak the Japanese good.

4. Even though it hot today, but I want eat ice cream.

5. Every students don't like test.

6. Please turn the light. It is dark too much at here.

7. I will tomorrow go to shopping in downtown.

8. I play sometimes ski at winter.

9. He like draw painting, so maybe he will an artist.

10. She can't do drive a car because she is young too much.

Grammar Focus 7

ALL OF THE SENTENCES BELOW HAVE MISTAKES. TRY TO CORRECT THE SENTENCES, AND MAKE THEM **PERFECT**.

1. News on TV were very interest and excited.

2. I can't go to a trip in May 15 because I had better to study.

3. Almost people enjoy to play the soccer at summer time.

4. Each boys and girl want to play piano.

5. She study hard the test, so she pass a test.

6. I ready to take trip in Kyoto on bus.

7. When I waked in yesterday, there was sunny outside.

8. I saw him fell down, so I helped to him.

9. A elephant is largest animals in world.

10. I dislike to listen musics, but I sing very beautiful.

Grammar Focus 8

ALL OF THE SENTENCES BELOW HAVE MISTAKES. TRY TO CORRECT THE SENTENCES, AND MAKE THEM **PERFECT**.

1. She asked to him a question, and he don't know answer.

2. I always am tired in weekend.

3. My old, cute sister is lived at New York.

4. My dog is liking play games to me.

5. At the night, he does a bath for clean his body.

6. He have many money, but he car is an expensive.

7. I am thinking that you are a friend person.

8. I have lived at my home since 4 years.

9. Play games is funny, especially on the park.

10. It is a flower on the wood, small, yellow table.

Grammar Focus 9

ALL OF THE SENTENCES BELOW HAVE MISTAKES. TRY TO CORRECT THE SENTENCES, AND MAKE THEM **PERFECT**.

1. If it will rainy tomorrow, I bring a umbrella.

2. As soon as I woke up today morning, I washing my face.

3. In morning, he eat sometimes a pizza.

4. She can do swim very fastly.

5. I am wanting new computer, but I am no money.

6. He foot smell nicely.

7. Two day ago, I wash my a uniform, so now it clean.

8. At the middle in a mountain, I looked bear.

9. If I am a dog, I sleep on a bed.

10. Where my book is? I can't finding it somewhere.

Grammar Focus 10

1. In Internet, you can getting many informations about world.

2. She don't know where is her car, so she call police.

3. Last time I played guitar, my mom gots angry to me.

4. I enjoy to meet the people, so people says I am friendly guy.

5. Tomorrow's night, I do my computer.

6. I looked a movie the last week, and it was a funny.

7. When I eat a rice, I use always a chopstick.

8. I am owning many furnitures.

9. Please send to me a email about your trip to USA.

10. That pants look good at you. Where did you buy it?

Grammar Focus 11

ALL OF THE SENTENCES BELOW HAVE MISTAKES. TRY TO CORRECT THE SENTENCES, AND MAKE THEM **PERFECT**.

1. Next times I will go to shopping, I bought a milk.

2. I don't have no magazine about car.

3. I eat myself, so I sometimes am feeling alone.

4. It book is interested, so I want really buy it.

5. My tall, funny friend like to watching the TV.

6. I not good in painting, but my sister do.

7. Canada is second big country in the world. Russia is more bigger Canada.

8. Almost people in that family speaks English good. They is smart.

9. Before come to here, please to do your homeworks careful.

10. Monkey live on tree, and bear sleep on a cave.

Grammar Focus 12

1. She is good tennis, so she is strong leg.

2. It is bored to studying sometimes English.

3. I forgot doing my works, so my teacher yelled to me.

4. Please stop to talk! I watch a movie right now.

5. My birthday was in March 17, and I like to do parties.

6. If I am the bird, I will eat the bug.

7. We study at 4 to 5:20 at this room in 3rd floor.

8. At the first, I don't like dog, but now I think it is cute.

9. I dislike to eat a chicken because it is smell bad..

10. Almost every people in this class have a black hair.

Grammar Focus 13

ALL OF THE SENTENCES BELOW HAVE MISTAKES. TRY TO CORRECT THE SENTENCES, AND MAKE THEM **PERFECT**.

1. Each of my pen in my pencil's case are blue.

2. I am believing she is beautifulest girl in world.

3. In top of the SES Library, it is an nice room for study.

4. His car is more bigger my car, so I am jealous at him.

5. She is more loudly than me, but I still liking she.

6. Yesterday, I meet several of people at restaurant.

7. He eat a fish every day, because he like to do fishing.

8. Toyota is the most big car's company in Japan.

9. You had better to not play guitar late night.

10. They won't not take a travel to America the next week.

Grammar Focus 14

1. At summer, I might be go to a trip with my family's member.

2. On July, I will going to buy new phone, because mine old.

3. I get B in test yesterday, so I am feeling happy.

4. My pen is made by plastic, at Mexican, from Parker Company.

5. When I angry, I stop talk and left the room fastly.

6. It take me one hour and half come here by a bus.

7. I have to yesterday finish to do my homeworks, but I can't.

8. Many of persons in USA has 2 car.

9. The moon colour is yellow colour like a cheese.

10. I must to help my friend because he is trouble.

Grammar Focus 15

1. My mom hitted me at a leg because I was unkind at her..

2. I am shopping every day, so I am not money.

3. If I am monkey, I eat banana.

4. Don't let your dog to eat the chocolate too many.

5. In morning, I am watching news on the TV every day.

6. I bought a clothes 3 day ago for my friend wedding.

7. I wish I can speak Chinese language.

8. I must to finishing my homeworks.

9. At my birthday, many my friend buy to me present.

10. When weather is cool, many of people riding a bike.

Prepositions
Section

Prepositions 1

FILL IN THE BLANK: WRITE A PROPER PREPOSITION FOR EACH SENTENCE. SOMETIMES, THERE IS MORE THAN ONE ANSWER. ALSO, PREPOSITIONS ARE USED IN IDIOMS. THESE PHRASAL VERBS MUST BE MEMORIZED.

1. The pen _____ my hand was made _____ China.

2. _____ Christmas Day, people open _____ presents.

3. _____ TV, I watched a movie _____ elephants.

4. I am bad _____ computer games. I always see the words GAME _____.

5. I hope I don't look _____ a monster _____ space.

6. If you look _____ the window, you can see a gorilla hanging _____ a tree.

7. We study _____ 1 hour and a half _____ this office.

8. The boy studies _____ school _____ 9am _____ 3pm.

9. Get _____ the car, or get _____ the bus. But please hurry _____.

10. _____ first, I didn't like fish, but now I do.

11. I am writing _____ my book right now. I am writing _____ a pen.

12. A: Braklatikchar!   B: What are you talking _____?

13. I was born _____ March, _____ the morning, _____ a cold day.

14. Did you pay _____ your pants _____ cash?

15. My car is made _____ the Honda Car Company.

Prepositions 2

FILL IN THE BLANK: WRITE A PROPER PREPOSITION FOR EACH SENTENCE. SOMETIMES, THERE IS MORE THAN ONE ANSWER. ALSO, PREPOSITIONS ARE USED IN IDIOMS. THESE PHRASAL VERBS MUST BE MEMORIZED.

1. I usually go to work _____ foot, not _____ a car or _____ a horse.

2. _____ the weekend, I sometimes sleep _____ a long time.

3. He spoke _____ a deep voice. He sounds _____ a monster.

4. _____ 2020, the Olympics will be _____ Tokyo.

5. I am always nice _____ my dog. I give him steak _____ breakfast.

6. Really, I don't agree _____ you. My feet DON'T smell _____ fish.

7. He is afraid _____ snakes, so don't give him a snake _____ his birthday.

8. Can I borrow this book _____ you?

9. I have to go. I'm _____ a hurry. I am late _____ school.

10. Planes always fly _____ my house _____ the sky _____ Sunday morning.

11. He is training _____ a marathon. He is _____ good shape.

12. When people go _____ a wedding, they always dress _____ (wear nice clothes).

13. There is something wrong _____ my computer. Smoke is coming _____ _____ it.

14. Please write a story _____ a monster that looks _____ a rock.

15. _____ this moment, I am sitting _____ a chair and drinking a glass _____ water.

Prepositions 3

FILL IN THE BLANK: WRITE A PROPER PREPOSITION FOR EACH SENTENCE. SOMETIMES, THERE IS MORE THAN ONE ANSWER. ALSO, PREPOSITIONS ARE USED IN IDIOMS. THESE PHRASAL VERBS MUST BE MEMORIZED.

1. I am going to take a trip _____ France. See you _____ a month. Good-bye...

2. I am tired _____ washing dishes. I really don't like doing it.

3. The two boys had a fight _____ the last piece of candy.

4. If you jump _____ _____ an airplane, be careful.

5. Tissue is made _____ wood, and this table is made _____ wood.

6. Can you jump _____ a diving board?

7. I am jealous _____ people who are tall. I am too short.

8. Some people are terrified _____ animals.

9. Don't laugh _____ me. I fell _____ and got a cut _____ my knee.

10. The rocket took _____ _____ the morning. I wonder where it's going?

11. I studied hard _____ the test. I hope I get an A+ _____ the test.

12. Can you take a picture _____ me?

13. We play UNO _____ cards.

14. It's nice today. Let's go _____ and play _____ the park.

15. I am terrible _____ skiing. I prefer swimming _____ skiing.

Prepositions 4

FILL IN THE BLANK: WRITE A PROPER PREPOSITION FOR EACH SENTENCE. SOMETIMES, THERE IS MORE THAN ONE ANSWER. ALSO, PREPOSITIONS ARE USED IN IDIOMS. THESE PHRASAL VERBS MUST BE MEMORIZED.

1. Did you find what you were looking _____?

2. The house is _____ fire. Call the police.

3. The firemen are trying to put _____ the fire. I hope they can do it.

4. Turn _____ the radio. I want to listen _____ music.

5. I don't like tests _____ all, but I need to study _____ tests.

6. What's the matter _____ you? Why are you crying _____ a baby turtle?

7. Would you like a piece _____ pizza? I made it _____ myself.

8. I am interested _____ sports.

9. The bad guy escaped _____ the police. I saw him climbing _____ a wall.

10. What are you laughing _____?

11. Could you please move _____? I can't sit _____.

12. The dentist told me to open _____ my mouth.

13. I ate some bad food. Arrrrr…I feel terrible…I'm going to throw _____.

14. Do you sleep _____ pyjamas?

15. Please stop screaming. What's wrong? Calm _____.

Prepositions 5

FILL IN THE BLANK: WRITE A PROPER PREPOSITION FOR EACH SENTENCE. SOMETIMES, THERE IS MORE THAN ONE ANSWER. ALSO, PREPOSITIONS ARE USED IN IDIOMS. THESE PHRASAL VERBS MUST BE MEMORIZED.

1. _____ Sunday morning, I went _____ a store _____ car.

2. _____ Christmas, I went _____ a trip _____ a week.

3. I live very far _____ this building. I never come here _____ foot.

4. _____ the morning, I drink a cup _____ coffee _____ my friend.

5. _____ the Internet, I always read news _____ the world.

6. I was born _____ a hospital, _____ March 14, _____ 1971.

7. We study _____ 4 o'clock _____ 5:30 _____ Monday.

8. Please write your name _____ the top _____ this paper.

9. The lady drove _____ the bridge _____ a fast speed.

10. Get _____ the elevator. Let's go. Hurry _____.

11. I am looking _____ to meeting my friends _____ Friday night. It will be so much fun.

12. Spiderman can climb _____ walls and jump _____ cars. AMAZING!

13. The lights _____ this room are _____ our heads.

14. I need to go _____ a diet. Yesterday, I broke a chair.

15. What kind _____ pizza do you like?

Prepositions 6

1. I bought my computer _____ $900.

2. She grew _____ in a small town called Miniscule.

3. Always pay attention _____ your teachers, or they will get mad _____ you.

4. Our class starts _____ 4, and you came here _____ 4:30. You were not _____ time.

5. The test is _____. Please stop writing, and give your tests _____ me.

6. We dream _____ taking a holiday _____ Australia.

7. I had a dream _____ a dragon yesterday. It was scary.

8. _____ the top _____ the mountain, you can see my castle _____ the sky.

9. _____ the corner _____ this room, you can see a small table.

10. That shirt looks great _____ you. You should wear it _____ the party.

11. Thanks. I bought the shirt _____ sale. I paid $5 _____ it.

12. I live _____ a train station. It takes me 2 minutes _____ foot.

13. Can you forgive me _____ breaking your TV? I didn't do it _____ purpose.

14. Thank you _____ helping me fix my toilet. You are very kind.

15. It's raining today, so let's stay _____ the house and watch a movie _____ TV.

Prepositions 7

FILL IN THE BLANK: WRITE A PROPER PREPOSITION FOR EACH SENTENCE. SOMETIMES, THERE IS MORE THAN ONE ANSWER. ALSO, PREPOSITIONS ARE USED IN IDIOMS. THESE PHRASAL VERBS MUST BE MEMORIZED.

1. _____ the end _____ the month, I always clean _____ my room.

2. Your feet are _____ the table, and your socks smell _____ onions.

3. This book belongs _____ me. See, my name is _____ the cover.

4. This movie is boring. I'm going to turn it _____.

5. _____ the middle _____ the night, my telephone rang.

6. So, I picked _____ the phone and talked _____ my mom _____ 1 hour.

7. What are you upset _____? I broke your pen _____ accident.

8. _____ water, all plants can't live.

9. _____ the sky, birds sometimes fly _____ my head.

10. The ghost walked _____ the door, sat _____, and started to sing a song _____ bugs.

11. Once _____ a time, there was a princess named Elizabeth.

12. Princess Elizabeth lived _____ a castle _____ her parents and 4 brothers.

13. The princess wanted to take a trip _____ the world, but her parents said NO.

14. So one day, she climbed _____ her window and escaped _____ the castle alone.

15. She is traveling right now, and her parents are very worried _____ her.

Prepositions 8

FILL IN THE BLANK: WRITE A PROPER PREPOSITION FOR EACH SENTENCE. SOMETIMES, THERE IS MORE THAN ONE ANSWER. ALSO, PREPOSITIONS ARE USED IN IDIOMS. THESE PHRASAL VERBS MUST BE MEMORIZED.

1. I am _____ Canada, and my birthday is _____ March.

2. I woke _____ _____ 6am today. Then I went _____ a walk.

3. My books are _____ the table, not _____ my bag.

4. The ceiling is _____ our heads.

5. The computer is made _____ Apple.

6. We study _____ 1 _____ 2.

7. _____ TV, there is a lot _____ news _____ the weather.

8. Do you want to eat lunch _____ me?

9. I borrowed this book _____ the library.

10. I came here _____ car, not _____ foot or _____ a car.

11. She takes medicine _____ her headaches.

12. What is the difference _____ afraid and scared?

13. I bought my coat _____ a department store. It was _____ sale.

14. Put _____ your hat, and let's go _____ the restaurant.

15. _____ Christmas, I always call my mom.

Prepositions 9

FILL IN THE BLANK: WRITE A PROPER PREPOSITION FOR EACH SENTENCE. SOMETIMES, THERE IS MORE THAN ONE ANSWER. ALSO, PREPOSITIONS ARE USED IN IDIOMS. THESE PHRASAL VERBS MUST BE MEMORIZED.

1. The number 5 is _____ 4 and 6.

2. He is good _____ singing, so he wants to be _____ a band.

3. He eats food _____ chopsticks (箸), not _____ his hands.

4. She is interested _____ movies, so maybe she wants to be _____ a movie.

5. She comes here _____ a bicycle. Biking is good _____ her health.

6. He got _____ a bus, and after 10 minutes, he got _____ the bus.

7. I wouldn't like to live _____ a tiger.

8. She designed (設計) the building _____ herself. She has talent.

9. I lived _____ Monkey Island _____ 2 years.

10. My friend looks _____ her mom, so her mom is happy _____ that.

11. I saw him standing _____ the bus stop.

12. She visited many shrines (神社) _____ her trip _____ Tokyo.

13. I got a B _____ the test.

14. Why are you yelling _____ him?

15. Her guitar is made _____ wood, and it was made _____ the USA.

Prepositions 10

FILL IN THE BLANK: WRITE A PROPER PREPOSITION FOR EACH SENTENCE. SOMETIMES, THERE IS MORE THAN ONE ANSWER. ALSO, PREPOSITIONS ARE USED IN IDIOMS. THESE PHRASAL VERBS MUST BE MEMORIZED.

1. _____ the morning, I am always _____ a hurry, so I eat breakfast _____ my car.

2. Thank you _____ helping me _____ these heavy bags.

3. I give _____. I don't know the answer.

4. *Yesterday* is a song _____ the Beatles.

5. She is talented _____ painting.

6. This morning, I _____-slept, so I was late _____ the meeting.

7. _____ fact, I have 3 helicopters. Are you surprised _____ that?

8. Could you turn _____ the volume? I can't hear the TV.

9. She was _____ to move to Hawaii, but she decided not to go.

10. I waited _____ 2 hours. _____ last, she came to the coffee shop.

11. My computer is made _____ Apple.

12. The coffee shop is _____ top _____ the building.

13. _____ 4 hours, I will finish my job and go home _____ bus.

14. I want to talk to you _____ your shoes. They smell _____ natto.

15. The sky is dark. I think it is _____ to rain.

Prepositions 11

FILL IN THE BLANK: WRITE A PROPER PREPOSITION FOR EACH SENTENCE. SOMETIMES, THERE IS MORE THAN ONE ANSWER. ALSO, PREPOSITIONS ARE USED IN IDIOMS. THESE PHRASAL VERBS MUST BE MEMORIZED.

1. Because _____ the storm, many people stayed _____ their homes.

2. I like to draw _____ paper _____ my pencil.

3. When I drive my car, I always put _____ my seatbelt.

4. _____ summer, many people eat _____ restaurants _____ their friends.

5. Her drawer was full _____ stuff made _____ China.

6. He is fantastic _____ singing, and he dances _____ a pro.

7. I am bored _____ this book.

8. She likes shopping _____ clothes.

9. I have never flown _____ a helicopter because I am afraid _____ helicopters.

10. I forgot _____ the test. I am _____ BIG trouble.

11. There is a restaurant _____ the 10th floor _____ that building.

12. There are many stars _____ space.

13. Babies grow _____ _____ their clothes fast.

14. There are many nice homes _____ the river. Maybe they are expensive.

15. She always takes care _____ her family, so everybody loves her.

Prepositions 12

WRITE A PROPER PREPOSITION FOR EACH SENTENCE. SOMETIMES, THERE IS MORE THAN ONE ANSWER. ALSO, PREPOSITIONS ARE USED IN IDIOMS. THESE PHRASAL VERBS MUST BE MEMORIZED.

1. Don't jump _____ the water. It's freezing cold.

2. What did you have _____ supper last night?

3. If you need help _____ your work, send an e-mail _____ me.

4. The robber stole money _____ the bank. Now, the police are looking _____ him.

5. She hit me _____ the leg because I broke her watch _____ accident.

6. He was _____ a car accident. Luckily, he is okay.

7. I am allergic _____ soap, so I don't smell so good.

8. The picnic was called _____ because it was raining hard.

9. The boy jumped _____ his bed, and landed _____ the ground.

10. This book was written _____ a man _____ a moustache _____ his face.

11. In Russia, there are _____ (more than) 10 000 lakes.

12. I hope you always wash your hands _____ soap.

13. He lent a book _____ his friend, but the friend didn't give it _____.

14. She is crazy _____ music. She listens to music, even _____ the shower.

15. _____ time _____ time, I go to a movie theatre.

Prepositions 13

FILL IN THE BLANK: WRITE A PROPER PREPOSITION FOR EACH SENTENCE. SOMETIMES, THERE IS MORE THAN ONE ANSWER. ALSO, PREPOSITIONS ARE USED IN IDIOMS. THESE PHRASAL VERBS MUST BE MEMORIZED.

1. Before I sleep, I always turn _____ the lights.

2. I made this cake _____ you. I hope you aren't allergic _____ chocolate.

3. I am excited _____ the concert next week. I can't wait _____ go.

4. I live _____ the 3rd floor, and I always walk _____ and _____ the stairs.

5. The moon flies _____ the earth.

6. He never has a smile _____ his face. He always looks angry.

7. I have the same name _____ my grandfather.

8. She came here _____ her mom. After class, they will go shopping _____ clothes.

9. Open _____ the window. It's really hot _____ here.

10. She painted that picture _____ colour because she prefers colour _____ black and white.

11. Before you walk _____ the street, check _____ cars.

12. _____ mountains, always be careful _____ bears and monkeys.

13. Are you happy _____ your new phone?

14. I have a question _____ you. Do you like bugs?

15. I'm not happy today. I really feel _____. Please cheer me _____.

Prepositions 14

1. I like to read books _____ magic.

2. You must run _____ _____ here. The building is _____ fire.

3. I have worked here _____ 3 years.

4. I put my money _____ a piggy bank. I want to buy a hat made _____ gold.

5. Be careful _____ the baby. Don't drop her _____ the ground.

6. I sent a letter _____ my mom, but I put the wrong address _____ the envelope.

7. Do you want to share this sandwich _____ me?

8. She always comes _____ class early. She likes to be _____ time.

9. The man fell _____, but he wasn't hurt _____ all.

10. She went to a sleep-_____ party, and she didn't sleep _____ 1am.

11. He talked _____ and _____ about his vacation. He talked a lot.

12. There is a hospital _____ _____ _____ this building.

13. The red team won the soccer game _____ 5 goals.

14. _____ the airplane, a fat man sat _____ _____ me.

15. _____ summer, birds fly _____ the sky and ducks swim _____ lakes.

73

Prepositions 15

FILL IN THE BLANK: WRITE A PROPER PREPOSITION FOR EACH SENTENCE. SOMETIMES, THERE IS MORE THAN ONE ANSWER. ALSO, PREPOSITIONS ARE USED IN IDIOMS. THESE PHRASAL VERBS MUST BE MEMORIZED.

1. Hurry _____ and tie _____ your shoes or you'll be late _____ school.

2. I sometimes think _____ my future. I hope it is good.

3. I like the taste _____ ketchup very much, so I always put some _____ my french fries.

4. Please throw _____ your stinky shoes. They smell _____ durians.

5. He plays _____ a soccer team, but the team is _____ last place. They aren't so good.

6. He went _____ with his friends, and came home late _____ night.

7. You must watch _____ _____ bears _____ mountains.

8. I saw a boy hit another boy _____ the leg _____ a stick. OUCH!

9. "Wake _____. You have a test _____ 30 minutes," my mom yelled.

10. I ran _____ the door, got _____ a taxi, and ran _____ the classroom.

11. But there was nobody _____ the room. I was confused.

12. I went _____ my home _____ foot. I walked _____ 2 hours.

13. _____ home, my mom was washing the dishes _____ a towel.

14. I said, "Mom, nobody was _____ school. I'm going to be _____ trouble."

15. She said, "Don't worry. I was joking _____ the test. It's tomorrow. Hahahahaha."

Articles Section

Articles 1

It was _____ hot day_____ last Friday, so I went to _____ pool near my house. It is near _____ park. I am _____ good swimmer, but I'm not _____ best swimmer in _____ my family.

_____ next day, I went to _____ Haru Beach, very close to _____ Reo Highway. After swimming at _____ beach, I went to _____ movie theatre, and watched _____ movie called "Help".

After _____ movie, I went to _____ hotel. I went to _____ Yura Hotel to eat _____ dinner at _____ restaurant in _____ hotel. _____ food was good, so I'll go there again _____ next week. After eating, I went to _____ Emi Mountain by _____ car.

Next week, I might go to _____ Hiro River, or _____ Lake Yuri. I might even take _____ tour of _____ Europe.

Articles 2

Fill in the blanks (a, an, the or X)

Articles are always used before nouns. Common singular nouns (i.e. a car, a chair, an apple) are the most common nouns to take articles. Proper nouns (i.e. The Hudson River) sometimes take the article THE, sometimes not. Non-counting nouns and plural nouns also take articles sometimes, if they are known to the speaker (i.e. The water in my glass is hot)

Once upon _____ time, there was _____ boy who was _____ only person in his family who could fly in _____ sky

like _____ bird. _____ boy was _____ 8 year old boy, and his father was _____ inventor. _____ father invented

_____ medicine that could change people into _____ birds.

One day, while _____ father was at _____ work in _____ Moonlife Building (he worked on _____ 10th floor in

_____ room 1007), _____ boy drank some of _____ magic liquid.

Suddenly, _____ boy started to fly in _____ room, then out _____ window, and then around _____ world at _____

fast speed. He flew past _____ Statue of Liberty, _____ New York City, _____ Gogaga Hall and _____ Yankee

Stadium. Then he crossed _____ Atlantic Ocean and flew past _____ Eiffel Tower. Next, he sped past _____ Great

Wall of China and _____ Mount Fuji. He got tired, so he rested in _____ Naka Park.

When he got home _____ hour late for _____ supper, his dad was so angry that he yelled at _____ boy for _____

week and _____ half. _____ boy was never allowed to leave _____ house, and he is still there now.

Articles 3

Fill in the blanks (a, an, the or X)
Articles are always used before nouns. Common singular nouns (i.e. a car, a chair, an apple) are the most common nouns to take articles. Proper nouns (i.e. The Hudson River) sometimes take the article THE, sometimes not. Non-counting nouns and plural nouns also take articles sometimes, if they are known to the speaker (i.e. The water in my glass is hot)

In _____ world, there are many strange _____ animals, and one of _____ strangest is _____ bat. _____ bat eats

mostly _____ bugs, so _____ people who live near _____ bats are usually very happy. _____ Bat is blind, and it

sees by using its voice. _____ Bat lives in _____ cave, like _____ Fregosi Caves in _____ Italy, and they live in

_____ group, not alone.

One time, _____ bat came into my home, and my father was _____ angry man. That was _____ first time I ever

saw him so mad. He picked up _____ broom, and chased _____ bat for half _____ hour. Finally, _____ bat flew out

_____ window in _____ kitchen, and we all felt _____ lot happier.

_____ Bat is not _____ dangerous animal, but people are _____ little afraid of them. Some bats drink _____ blood.

They are called vampire bats, but they cannot change into _____ vampire, so don't worry.

Articles 4

I like to ask students questions.

If ____ student doesn't know _____ answer to ____ question, I never get angry. If ____ question is too difficult

for _____ student, I always ask ____ question again. If ____ student still doesn't understand _____ question,

then I ask ____ different, easier question. I just want ____ student to speak. That is my job.

Have ___ nice day. And please do _____ homework I give you on _____ weekend. Then you will be _____ good

English speaker, and I will be _____ happiest teacher in _____ world.

Articles 5

_____ First time my family bought _____ TV, I was such _____ happy boy. It was _____ small TV, made by _____ Sony company, and it was made in _____ United States. It was _____ color TV.

On my tv, I could see _____ lives of people in _____ other countries.

In _____ China, I saw _____ Yellow River. In _____ Korea, I saw _____ Namsan Tower and _____ Han River. In Japan, I saw _____ Osaka Castle and _____ Fuji Mountain. In Africa, I saw _____ Pyramids. In Europe, I could see _____ Queen Elizabeth, _____ London Bridge, and _____ Louvre Museum in _____ city of Paris.

But there was ____ problem with having ____ TV. I stayed at _____ home too much. I stopped going outside. So, my mom threw _____ TV into _____ garbage after I got _____ F on _____ Math test.

Articles 6

1. _____ Lake Ontario is _____ very large lake.

2. _____ Pacific Ocean has many _____ sharks in it.

3. _____ Logan Mountain is _____ highest mountain in _____ North America.

4. _____ Nile River is long.

5. _____ Empire State Building has _____ zoo on _____ 1st floor.

6. _____ Naka Park is beside _____ Naka Hotel.

7. _____ Naka Museum has many paintings in it.

8. _____ Grand Canyon is filled with _____ rocks and _____ zebras.

9. _____ Yankee Stadium is famous in New York.

10. _____ Golden Gate Bridge was built in _____ 1960s.

Articles 7

1. _____ Cartoons on _____ STV always make me laugh.

2. _____ Han River has _____ lots of water and _____ fish in it.

3. In _____ Canada, you can go to _____ Pacific Ocean, or _____ USA by _____ car.

4. I have _____ same hat that you have.

5. He has _____ cold, so he went to _____ hospital.

6. When she goes to _____ school, her mom makes her _____ lunch.

7. _____ Elephant is _____ largest land animal in _____ Africa.

8. _____ Champlain Bridge was built in _____ 1960s.

9. _____ French language is not easy to learn.

10. _____ Narita Airport is very busy in _____ summer.

Articles 8

1. _____ next month, I'm going to buy _____ new bike.

2. Two years ago, I went to _____ Spain. _____ next year, I went to Brazil.

3. _____ First time I swam in _____ Black Sea, it was on _____ vacation.

4. Don't leave right now. We have to lock _____ front door.

5. _____ first time I met you, you were very quiet.

6. _____ Chinese like to take holidays in _____ USA.

7. _____ largest lake in _____ Japan is _____ Lake Biwa.

8. Only _____ few students failed _____ test, and one student got _____ B.

9. Many birds fly _____ south for _____ winter.

10. Do you have _____ pencil with _____ eraser? I lost mine in _____ Naka Library.

Articles 9

Rex

I bought _____ dog 3 weeks ago, _____ cute dog, and _____ dog's name is _____ Rex. It is _____ poodle, and we bought it at _____ Rockland Shopping Mall, and I paid _____ hundred dollars for _____ dog. When it is hungry, it goes into _____ kitchen, looking for _____ snack or _____ water.

_____ last week, we were walking in _____ Benny Park. I met _____ man with _____ same dog as Rex, _____ poodle. _____ Two dogs started to play with each other, and soon they were _____ friends.

_____ Next day, I met 2 _____ other people in _____ park. They were taking pictures for _____ magazine called _____ Puppylove.

They both wanted to take _____ picture of _____ Rex. I said yes. _____ Week later, I got _____ phone call from _____ owner of _____ magazine, and he told me that he wanted Rex to be in _____ movie. _____ movie's name was 'Super Poo,' and he wanted Rex to be _____ star in _____ movie.

I said yes. I got on _____ plane, and traveled to _____ USA. When _____ plane landed, I saw someone holding _____ sign, and _____ sign said, "Welcome Rex!" My dog is now _____ star.

Articles 10

1. I have _____ only one computer, and it is made by _____ Toshiba.

2. At _____ top of _____ Sharpy Hill, you can see _____ stars.

3. Yesterday, I took _____ shower and went for _____ walk.

4. _____ Boston Library is _____ oldest library in _____ America.

5. She is _____ only girl in _____ class, and she wears _____ nice uniform.

6. _____ Mount Everest is in _____ Himalayas.

7. I stayed at _____ Naka Hotel for _____ week.

8. _____ Naka Bridge was built in _____ 1940s.

9. You can find _____ South Pole in _____ Antarctica.

10. There is _____ clock in _____ London called _____ Big Ben.

Articles 11

Fill in the blanks (a, an, the or X)
Articles are always used before nouns. Common singular nouns (i.e. a car, a chair, an apple) are the most common nouns to take articles. Proper nouns (i.e. The Hudson River) sometimes take the article THE, sometimes not. Non-counting nouns and plural nouns also take articles sometimes, if they are known to the speaker (i.e. The water in my glass is hot)

The Queen's Problem

_____ Queen Miwa had _____ big problem.

She was _____ ruler of _____ Pukey Empire, and had _____ only one daughter, and her daughter was in _____ 4ᵗʰ grade. _____ queen's daughter's name was Ylgu. She was _____ intelligent girl who ate _____ apple and _____ orange every day, but she was not beautiful at _____ all. Miwa wanted her daughter to be _____ beauty queen, so she went to _____ doctor at _____ Miracle Hospital to make her daughter pretty.

_____ Doctor Hasome took _____ look at _____ daughter, and said he could give her _____ special medicine that might make her _____ most beautiful woman on _____ Earth. However, _____ medicine was very hard to make, and it would cost _____ lots of _____ money. In _____ world, there was _____ only one place where she could find _____ medicine, and this was in _____ Amazon Jungle. They needed to find _____ a special plant.

So, _____ Queen Miwa left right away on her boat. At _____ first, she didn't have _____ clue where to go, but she met _____ honest man who said he could give her _____ hand to find _____ plant. After _____ hour, they finally found _____ plant. It was in _____ pond. _____ Queen jumped into _____ water, but suddenly, _____ alligator jumped up and ate her in one bite. Sadly, _____ princess is still ugly, still waiting for her mom, and she is still studying hard.

Articles 12

Fill in the blanks (a, an, the or X)
Articles are always used before nouns. Common singular nouns (i.e. a car, a chair, an apple) are the most common nouns to take articles. Proper nouns (i.e. The Hudson River) sometimes take the article THE, sometimes not. Non-counting nouns and plural nouns also take articles sometimes, if they are known to the speaker (i.e. The water in my glass is hot)

1. _____ World War II was _____ long time ago.

2. If you go to _____ Atlantic Ocean, you can see _____ plenty of _____ whales.

3. I bought _____ Nintendo DS from _____ Nintendo Company _____ last month.

4. If you get _____ A on _____ test tomorrow, I will buy you _____ present.

5. On _____ July 1st, you should eat _____ rice and _____ spaghetti.

6. _____ Snow Festival in Sapporo is in _____ winter.

7. _____ Capital of _____ China is _____ Beijing.

8. I like _____ bread with _____ butter for _____ breakfast.

9. _____ More you study, _____ smarter you will be.

10. _____ Sate Family lives in _____ Sato Castle.

Articles 13

The Good Friend

Once upon _____ time, there lived _____ vampire who was such _____ nice guy that nobody believed that he was _____ vampire. _____ Vampire's name was Sang, and he lived with _____ friend of his who worked 7 days _____ week. The friend didn't have _____ lot of _____ money.

One day, Sang was watching _____ TV. On _____ news, he saw his friend in _____ police car. _____ policeman said that Sang's friend was _____ robber. The friend was going to _____ most terrible jail in _____ world.

Sang felt terrible, so he made _____ plan to rescue his _____ only friend..

Before Sang went to _____ jail, he changed into _____ bat, and started to fly at _____ very fast speed to _____ jail. It was _____ midnight when Sang arrived.

Sang landed on _____ roof as quietly as _____ mouse. Sang went to _____ 1st floor, and into _____ room with _____ lot of computers. He searched for his friend, and after half _____ hour, he found out that his friend was in _____ basement. He took _____ elevator to _____ basement, and when _____ doors opened, there were 50 guards waiting. Sang changed into _____ bat and flew to _____ room where his friend was. _____ Guards followed.

Sang smashed open _____ door, grabbed his friend, then smashed down _____ wall in the room. Sang changed into a super big bat. He picked up his friend, and they both flew away.

Articles 14

1. In _____ Olympics, many people try to win _____ gold medals.

2. He plays _____ piano very well.

3. Edison invented _____ light bulb in _____ 1879.

4. _____ police sometimes have to fight _____ bad guys.

5. _____ weather was nice yesterday.

6. The rocket flew into _____ space. It went to _____ moon.

7. At _____ Naka Station, I saw a man holding _____ umbrella.

8. He got _____ F on _____ test.

9. His mom was angry, so she hit him in _____ arm with _____ apple.

10. Please take _____ bath. You smell like _____ cheese.

Articles 15

_____ Funny thing happened to me while I was riding on _____ my new bike.

I was _____ only person riding on _____ Naka Street when _____ black cat walked across _____ road. I stopped _____ bike fast, but sadly, I ran over _____ cat's _____ tail.

_____ owner of _____ cat ran out of her house. She started to yell at me in _____ high voice. She was very _____ upset.

After _____ few minutes, _____ police car came along, and _____ policeman got out of _____ car. He was _____ only person in _____ car, and strangely, he had _____ only one eye. He asked _____ lady for _____ information about _____ accident.

She told him that she found _____ cat in _____ garbage. She was walking along _____ Naka River when _____ cat jumped onto her head. _____ cat jumped out of _____ garbage can. She took it back to her hotel, _____ Queeny Hotel, and then decided to bring it back home.

_____ Policeman looked at me angrily. I said, "Hey, it was _____ accident." But he didn't think so. He said, "You will have to give this lady _____ money to help _____ cat get better. Please give her _____ hundred dollars."

That's _____ lot of money, but I did it. I hope _____ cat and _____ lady and _____ policeman are happy. I'm not happy.

Eiken Practice

Eiken Practice 1

Circle the best answer.

1. You like pizza, _____?

    a) did you   b) can't you   c) don't you   d) will you

2. These gloves are too _____. Do you have bigger ones?

    a) ticklish   b) tight   c) talented   d) technical

3. A: I have a headache.   B: You should _____ some medicine.

    a) take   b) eat   c) make   d) sell

4. A: What do you think of my idea?   B: I think it _____ amazing.

    a) sounds   b) tastes   c) looks   d) feels

5. A: Would you like some coffee?   B: No thanks, I don't like coffee _____

    a) today   b) at all   c) of course   d) milk

6. When people cut _____ trees, it can destroy birds' nests.

    a) over   b) off   c) down   d) destroy

7. My friend is _____ at playing tennis. He's really bad.

    a) enjoys   b) horrible   c) talented   d) racket

8. I'm extremely busy. I don't think I can get there _____.

    a) for time   b) in time   c) by time   d) to time

9. I don't _____ so good. I think I'm going to go to bed. I think I have a cold. Ahhhh choooo.

    a) sound   b) taste   c) smell   d) feel

10. A: Would you like some coffee?   B: Well, I _____ water to coffee, if you don't mind.

    a) have   b) drink   c) like   d) prefer

Eiken Practice 2

Circle the best answer.

1. He graduated from Tokyo University, and started a large business. He is a _____.

    a) challenge   b) success   c) notice   d) detail

2. I was _____ by a dog when I was young. It was painful.

    a) walked   b) licked   c) had   d) attacked

3. I read in a book that mosquitoes are _____ to dark colors.

    a) interested   b) follow   c) bugs   d) attracted

4. A: Have you ever seen a _____?   B: No, and I don't want to.

    a) ghost   b) elevator   c) through   d) effort

5. The movie was great. The main _____ was really funny.

    a) popcorn   b) director   c) seat   d) actor

6. A: Did you watch the baseball game yesterday?   B: No, I'm not a _____ of baseball.

    a) game   b) understand   c) player   d) fan

7. My dog is _____ jumping over a chair. It's amazing.

    a) capable of   b) can   c) allowed to   d) effort

8. Leia is 14 years old. She studies at a good _____.

    a) time   b) kindergarten   c) university   d) high school

9. I thought it would rain today, but the weather _____ nice.

    a) played out   b) took out   c) walked out   d) turned out

10. I am not used to _____ tennis. I haven't played in many years.

    a) play   b) played   c) playing   d) must play

Eiken Practice 3

Circle the best answer.

1. Could you help me _____ for my hat? I think I lost it.

    a) find   b) pack   c) search   d) drill

2. I have never _____ this song before. It's great.

    a) listened   b) heard   c) sing   d) dance

3. Why did you kick my car? You _____ the door.

    a) fumbled   b) fought   c) dragged   d) damaged

4. Your party was great. The food was delicious, the music was nice, and the guests were_____.

    a) interest   b) interesting   c) interested   d) interviewed

5. Last night, I _____ my door wasn't locked, so I locked it before I went to bed.

    a) moved   b) noticed   c) pressed   d) peeped

6. Please _____ your hand if you have a question.

    a) pull   b) announce   c) raise   d) attend

7. I don't like to _____ tests.

    a) cheat on   b) pass by   c) take up   d) throw up

8. I _____ winter. I really like summer more.

    a) illike   b) unlike   c) relike   d) dislike

9. The baby fell _____ after I sang a song.

    a) down   b) awkward   c) asleep   d) sick

10. We have studied 25 minutes _____, and we have 35 minutes left.

    a) at all   b) so far   c) as long as   d) as soon as

Eiken Practice 3

Read the story and answer the questions.

The Tree and the Cloud

It was a hot summer day. For 2 months, it didn't rain, so the plants, trees, animals, and people in the Joojoo Forest were very unhappy and thirsty. When people, plants, trees and animals are thirsty, they want to drink something. And water is what they really, really want.

There was a queen tree in the forest, and her name was Queen Hihi. She was the tallest tree in the forest. Everybody liked her, and many animals and plants asked her for water.

"Please," they asked Hihi, "give us some water." And Hihi always helped them. She gave them her water everyday. Soon, Hihi was very thirsty. She didn't have a lot of water to give.

Remember that Hihi was a tall tree. She was so tall that at the top, she almost touched clouds in the sky.

One day, Hihi saw a cloud that was flying low. She was excited. When the cloud passed Hihi, she asked the cloud a question.

Hihi asked, " Cloud, why are you so sad?"

The cloud answered, "I am not sad."

But Hihi asked again. She said, "No, really, you look so sad. What happened? I think something bad happened to you."

The cloud thought and thought and thought again. Finally, the cloud remembered a sad memory.

"Yes, you are right," said the cloud. "I am soooooooooo sad," and the cloud started to cry and cry and cry.

Soon, the forest was covered with the cloud's rain. Everybody was happy...except the cloud.

Questions

1.   Why was everybody sad?

_____

2.   How was the weather in the forest?

_____

3. When trees are thirsty, what do they want to drink?

_____

4. How did Hihi make the cloud cry?

_____

5. How was Hihi able to talk to the cloud?

_____

Eiken Practice 5

Short essay. In 80-100 words, please write an essay on this topic:

Do you think students should go to school on Saturday?

_____

_____

_____

_____

_____

_____

_____

_____

_____

_____

_____

_____

_____

_____

_____

_____

_____

_____

Eiken Practice 6

Short essay. In 80-100 words, please write an essay on this topic:

Recycling is a waste of time and money.

_____

_____

_____

_____

_____

_____

_____

_____

_____

_____

_____

_____

_____

_____

_____

_____

_____

Eiken Practice 7

Circle the best answer.

1. I'm really tired. I think I'll _____ a nap.
   a) do   b) take   c) go   d) be

2. It is _____ cold outside. I want to stay inside.
   a) a little   b) much   c) many   d) too

3. You have 10 _____ on your feet.
   a) fingers   b) toes   c) elbows   d) stinky

4. A baby's skin _____ very soft.
   a) sounds   b) feels   c) smells   d) hears

5. I don't like spaghetti. _____ fact, I never eat it.
   a) in   b) on   c) at   d) by

6. _____ the night, I heard a strange sound...maybe a ghost?
   a) as soon as   b) when   c) during   d) while

7. I have almost 0 water in my cup. I have just _____ water.
   a) a little   b) a few   c) many   d) much

8. How _____ erasers do you have?
   a) are   b) do   c) many   d) much

9. I drank a _____ of juice yesterday.
   a) bag   b) can   c) piece   d) apple

10. A giraffe is _____ than a horse.
    a) taller   b) neck   c) dirtier   d) ride

Eiken Practice 8

Circle the best answer.

1. _____ people in the world don't like hospitals.
   a) Every   b) Most   c) Worries   d) Talented

2. My birthday is _____ March 14.
   a) in   b) fun   c) at   d) on

3. It's hard to _____ the word spaghetti.
   a) spell   b) say   c) digest   d) perform

4. Please hurry. We don't have _____ time.
   a) much   b) many   c) more   d) out of

5. _____ is before summer.
   a) ice cream   b) winter   c) spring   d) fall

6. Emma and Toma are young, _____, they can drive cars
   a) even though   b) as though   c) if   d) however

7. _____ Leia was watching tv, her friend called her.
   a) as soon as   b) during   c) while   d) when

8. It is cloudy outside. I think it might rain _____.
   a) next   b) soon   c) before   d) early

9. He waited for 3 hours for his friend. _____ last, his friend came.
   a) in   b) on   c) at   d) from

10. I just bought a new painting, but I'm not sure where I'm going to put it _____.
    a) on   b) over   c) for   d) up

BONUS QUESTION

11. This is the _____ question on this page.
    a) easy   b) easier   c) easiest   d)   most easy

Making Perfect Questions

MPQ 1

For each sentence, write a question that answers it.

For example, if the sentence is "I brush my teeth 3 times a day", the question could be "How often do you brush your teeth?" Many questions can be used for each sentence.

1. Seven.

2. On Saturday.

3. For 5 minutes.

4. I might go bowling tomorrow.

5. No, I won't.

6. He's over there.

7. Purple.

8. Because it's raining.

MPQ 2

For each sentence, write a question that answers it.

1. No, he couldn't.

2. Because I hurt my foot.

3. I think it's my eraser.

4. I want to eat the smaller one, please.

5. It's really delicious.

6. Under the table.

7. Like garbage.

8. D-I-C-T-I-O-N-A-R-Y

9. Around 10pm.

10. That's a funny question.

MPQ 3

For each sentence, write a question that answers it.

1. Kakakakakakaka.

2. He told me to sit down.

3. I go shopping one time a week.

4. I got an A on the test.

5. Yes, they are.

6. She is sleeping.

7. I exercise every morning.

8. Because he didn't study.

9. Never.

10. I didn't know that.

MPQ 4

For each sentence, write a question that answers it.

1. Yes, it does.

_____

2. I brush my teeth with a toothbrush.

_____

3. She is in the hospital.

_____

4. At 5pm.

_____

5. He studied at Harvard University.

_____

6. He has 2 children.

_____

7. In the bag.

_____

8. She will leave the hospital in 3 days.

_____

9. Because I have no money.

_____

10. No, it isn't.

_____

MPQ 5

1. She was studying.

2. Yes, I might.

3. I don't know.

4. He goes fishing every Sunday.

5. We will study 1 hour more.

6. I came here by horse.

7. Ice cream.

8. Her face is oval.

9. That shirt looks great on you.

10. That pink pencil case .

MPQ 6

For each sentence, write a question that answers it.

1. Only in the morning.

2. I have no umbrellas.

3. I got a book for my birthday.

4. His feet.

5. Yes, I have.

6. Russia is the biggest country in the world.

7. I can speak 3 languages.

8. Yesterday.

9. I am 175 cm tall.

10. I won't help you because you didn't help me.

MPQ 7

1. I live 10 minutes from here.

2. No, she can't.

3. What did you ask me?

4. Monkeys.

5. I have never been to the moon.

6. Sometimes, but not always.

7. I paid $5 for my book.

8. I met him at her party.

9. I didn't wake up until 10am.

10. I weigh about 85 kg.

MPQ 8

For each sentence, write a question that answers it.

---

1. Today is June 02.

---

2. I may go to my friend's home this weekend.

---

3. It's called *boshi* (hat) in Japanese.

---

4. No, I didn't.

---

5. She is a doctor.

---

6. I would like to buy a new car.

---

7. Please, don't ask me about that.

---

8. I swim very well.

---

9. Her hair is blond.

---

10. She looks like a smart girl.

Making Perfect Sentences

MPS 1

Write a sentence using each word.

nicely	
young	
Canadian	
silly	
every time	
below	
ham	
doctor	
long	
yellow	

MPS 2

Write a sentence using each word.

car	
the next time	
into	
ocean	
kind	
drive	
want	
horrible	
watch	
slowly	

MPS 3

Write a sentence using each word.

sometimes	
chair	
drop	
hard	
hardly	
however	
therefore	
as fun as	
important	
if it rains tomorrow	

MPS 4

Write a sentence using each word.

I would like to	
I used to	
over	
an (2x)	
a (2x)	
these	
because	
miss	
hope to	
I use	

MPS 5

Write a sentence using each word.

get	
several	
for	
3 days ago	
in 2hours	
after class	
arrive	
go shopping	
last week	
when I was young	

MPS 6

Write a sentence using each word.

right now	
next year	
soon	
before I go to school	
in the past	
no	
any	
every	
with	
without	

MPS 7

Write a sentence using each word.

early	
glad	
smelly	
some	
now	
another	
terrible	
easily	
fabulous	
almost	

MPS 8

Write a sentence using each word.

lost	
witch	
except	
turtle	
information	
furniture	
chicken	
salt	
water	
money	

MPS 9

Write a sentence using each word.

at	
from	
through	
along	
next to	
tall	
the nicest	
as fast as	
shorter	
more fun	

MPS 10

Write a sentence using each word.

word	
think	
even though	
hug	
bitter	
sweet	
sour	
none of	
five	
always	
almost never	

MPS 11

some of	
until	
once	
such a	
sandwich	
quite	
too	
sing	
ask	
lend	

MPS 12

Write a sentence using each word.

sell	
cut	
do	
tell	
search	
find	
give	
borrow	
buy	
take	

MPS 13

Write a sentence using each word.

come	
dance	
drink	
escape	
forget	
help	
drive	
kick	
let	
make	

MPS 14

Write a sentence using each word.

need	
stop	
wish	
hope	
join	
laugh	
like	
meet	
rest	
talk	

MPS 15

Write a sentence using each word.

angry	
calm	
exciting	
flat	
great	
important	
discuss	
large	
bored	
dirty	

MPS 16

Write a sentence using each word.

talented	
bored	
tired	
excited	
fascinated	
satisfied	
surprised	
exhausted	
pleased	
relaxed	

MPS 17

Write a sentence using each word.

amazing	
interesting	
exciting	
tiring	
charming	
boring	
frightening	
surprising	
disgusting	
annoying	

MPS 18

doctor	
teacher	
chef	
city	
park	
street	
pencil	
computer	
happiness	
love	

MPS 19

and	
but	
so	
or	
because of	
as soon as	
when	
every time	
while	
at first	

MPS 20

Write a sentence using each word.

first	
once	
twice	
a lot of	
next	
a few	
many	
much	
a great deal of	
last	

Writing: Short Stories

Short Story 1

A VERY BAD DAY

Short Story 2

MY BEST FRIEND

Short Story 3

THE MAGIC PENCIL

Short Story 4

LOST

Short Story 5

MY NEW HOME

Short Story 6

ROCKET SHOES

Short Story 7

GROW GROW GROW OH NO

Short Story 8

Writing: Essays

Essay 1

WINTER IS BETTER THAN SUMMER.

Essay 2

CHILDREN SHOULD NOT HAVE A SUMMER VACATION.

Essay 3

WATCHING TV IS GOOD FOR PEOPLE.

Essay 4

VIDEO/COMPUTER GAMES ARE BAD FOR PEOPLE.

Appendix

LIST OF PREPOSITIONS

Prepositions are words that tells us about where something is, or when something happens. They are always used to talk about nouns, like **on** TV, **in** my hand, or **above** my head. Here is a list of common prepositions:

aboard	about	above	across	After	against
ahead of	all over	along	among	Apart	around
as	At	away	away from	Back	before
behind	below	beneath	between	beyond	by
close by	close to	despite	down	during	except
for	forward	from	in	in between	in front of
inside	into	like	near	next to	of
off	on	on top of	opposite	outside	onto
over	out	out of	round	Past	since
through	to	toward	towards	under	until
upon	up	with	within	without	

OSASCNM – THE ORDER OF ADJECTIVES

In English, you must use adjectives in the certain order in a sentence. You must not mix up the order of the adjectives. It is one of English grammar rules.

If you can remember OSASCNM, then you will know the order of adjectives.

O = Opinion, **S** = Size, **A** = Age, **S** = Shape, **C** = Colour, **N** = Nationality, **M** = Material

◎ I have a <u>nice</u>, <u>big</u>, <u>old</u>, <u>square</u>, <u>brown</u>, <u>Canadian</u>, <u>wooden</u> chair.
      O   S   A   S   C   N   M

× I have a <u>big</u>, <u>square</u>, <u>Canadian</u>, <u>old</u>, <u>brown</u>, <u>nice</u> <u>wooden</u> chair.
     S   S   N   A   C   O   M

LIST OF IRREGULAR VERBS

Infinitive	Simple Past	Past Participle
be	was/were	been
beat	beat	beaten
become	became	become
begin	began	begun
bet*	bet	bet
blow	blew	blown
break	broke	broken
bring	brought	brought
build	built	built
buy	bought	bought
catch	caught	caught
choose	chose	chosen
come	came	come
cost	cost	cost
cut	cut	cut
deal	dealt	dealt
do	did	done
draw	drew	drawn
drink	drank	drunk
drive	drove	driven
eat	ate	eaten
fall	fell	fallen
feed	fed	fed
feel	felt	felt

Infinitive	Simple Past	Past Participle
fight	fought	fought
find	found	found
fly	flew	flown
forget	forgot	forgotten
freeze	froze	frozen
get	got	got, gotten
give	gave	given
go	went	gone
grow	grew	grown
hang	hung	hung
have	had	had
hear	heard	heard
hide	hid	hidden
hit	hit	hit
hold	held	held
hurt	hurt	hurt
keep	kept	kept
know	knew	known
lead	led	led
leave	left	left
lend	lent	lent
let	let	let
light*	lit	lit
lose	lost	lost
make	made	made
mean	meant	meant
meet	met	met

Infinitive	Simple Past	Past Participle
pay	paid	paid
put	put	put
read	read	read
ride	rode	ridden
ring	rang	rung
rise	rose	risen
run	ran	run
say	said	said
see	saw	seen
sell	sold	sold
send	sent	sent
set	set	set
shake	shook	shaken
steal	stole	stolen
shine	shone	shone
shoot	shot	shot
shut	shut	shut
sing	sang	sung
sink	sank	sunk
sit	sat	sat
sleep	slept	slept
slide	slid	slid
speak	spoke	spoken
spend	spent	spent
stand	stood	stood
stick	stuck	stuck
swear	swore	sworn

Infinitive	Simple Past	Past Participle
sweep	swept	swept
swim	swam	swum
swing	swung	swung
take	took	taken
teach	taught	taught
tear	tore	torn
tell	told	told
think	thought	thought
throw	threw	thrown
understand	understood	understood
wake*	woke	woken
wear	wore	worn
win	won	won
write	wrote	written